MOUNTED GAMES

Illustrations by
Carole Vincer

KENILWORTH PRESS

First published in Great Britain by
The Kenilworth Press Limited,
Addington, Buckingham, MK18 2JR

British Library Cataloguing in Publication Data
A catalogue record for this book is available from the British Library.

ISBN 1-872082-60-2

Typeset by The Kenilworth Press Limited

Printed in Great Britain by Westway Offset, Wembley

CONTENTS

Why mounted games are fun

Most riders start their competitive careers with some form of mounted games. Riding instructors often let their pupils relax by playing a mounted version of Grandmother's Footsteps: the young riders think it's fun, little realising that they are absorbing important lessons in controlling a pony as they vie to reach the instructor before she can catch them moving. Leading-rein classes in gymkhanas further encourage small novices to improve their co-ordination and balance.

Older children, with practice, can become very skilled at all types of mounted games and are enthusiastic participants in this form of competition. Even adults have been known to take part in open gymkhana events amid much giggling, groaning and general hilarity.

Why? The rewards are few and in all but the most important competitions – the Pony Club's Prince Philip Cup or the County Games Championships – success does not qualify you for anything. Prizes, if any, are small, and the rosettes awarded in gymkhana events are almost always the least spectacular.

The answer is that mounted games are relaxing, varied and, particularly in the case of team events, an excellent means of making friends. You do not need a cosseted show pony or have to worry unduly about strained tendons. Your mount can be a hairy monster or a shaggy bear. He can be ewe-necked, long-backed, narrow-chested or herring-gutted and you can still both enjoy yourselves without any hassle over turn-out or having to catch the judge's critical eye.

Mounted games really can be fun.

How mounted games began

Gymkhanas began in India in the days of the British Raj more than a century ago. Playing polo was a popular off-duty pastime of officers of British regiments stationed abroad, but informal competitions on horseback, such as tent-pegging, could be held in any open space and were just as relaxing.

Tent-pegging (pictured above) was – and still is – a fast and furious sport, requiring extraordinary skill and co-ordination. It remains popular in many countries to this day, and contests are regularly held.

In the days of the Raj other events could be enjoyed on any type of mount and, soon, wives and children clamoured to take part as well. Off-duty 'jollies' were organised, with races of various kinds, often over hurdles, laid on for everyone.

The Victoria Cross race, for example (below left), is still played today. The rider gallops across the arena where he picks up his 'wounded comrade' and together they ride to the finish. Dressing-up races were also popular, but the nineteenth-century version (below right) was more ambitious than its modern counterpart. Imagine riding side-saddle as fast as you can over hurdles, whilst carrying an umbrella!

When families returned to England, gymkhana games were introduced to liven up garden parties and fêtes. Before long, they became events in their own right, especially for children, who found their small ponies ideally suited to mounted games.

The ideal pony

Trying to describe the ideal mounted games pony is extremely difficult – so much depends on the pony's temperament and the physical build and athletic ability of the rider. It is, however, safe to say that the ideal pony should: (1) have a lively but unflappable temperament; (2) stand between 12.2 and 13.2 hands high; (3) have a good head carriage, deep girth and strong quarters; and (4) be eight years old or over.

Of all the attributes, **temperament** is probably the most important. A pony who can enter into the spirit of mounted games, enjoys competing and is unconcerned by the various pieces of equipment he is likely to meet, can be forgiven any number of conformation faults.

Size is governed by the build of the rider and the rules of official mounted games competitions. In the Pony Club, for example, the weight of the rider when dressed for competition may prevent a very small pony from being used. And as many games call for the rider to dismount and remount, it makes sense to choose a pony that is not too big. In fact, ponies over 14.2 hh are not allowed to take part in Pony Club games.

Otherwise, the general rule is that big ponies are faster than small ones, but small ponies may be more agile and easier to get on and off.

Alertness in a games pony is a sign that he enjoys the competition as much as his rider. The pony is clearly aware of everything that is going on and can't wait to join in.

Bending calls for **agility** and **suppleness** – many skilled games ponies carry out a series of flying changes as they speed in and out of the poles.

Age is immaterial, except that no pony under four years of age is allowed to take part in mounted games. The best pony, in fact, is at least eight years old. An older pony with experience, however, should never be ignored, and there are many excellent games ponies who are still competing at the highest level when they are well into their twenties. If you do choose an old pony, it is important to remember that he will need extra care and feeding.

Only some aspects of **conformation** are relevant. A good head carriage makes a pony easier to control as he is less likely to lean on the bit. It is also easier to vault onto a pony who keeps his head high. A deep girth and broad chest give plenty of lung room and suggest stamina. Strong quarters indicate natural impulsion and speed.

Undoubtedly, the smaller breeds of British native ponies are perfectly suited to mounted games. Perhaps that is why gymkhanas are so popular throughout the British Isles. They are not, however, show ponies, and there is many a brilliant games pony who would be laughed out of the show ring.

A good pony needs to be alert, supple, agile and obedient. At the very least, he should be physically capable, with schooling and practice, of acquiring all four attributes.

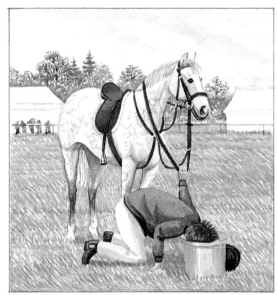

An **obedient** pony who will stand still while the rider concentrates on retrieving an apple or performs other intricate tasks will gain several valuable seconds.

Speed and **rhythm** are vital. This pony keeps straight as he approaches the flag, allowing his rider to grasp and remove it in one fluid movement.

Training the pony

A well-trained games pony moves easily from a standstill to a canter, stops on command and responds to neck-reining. As these are not part of normal schooling, mounted games ponies have to learn a different set of rules.

In a games competition, every second saved is a second gained and, instead of making a smooth progression up and down the paces, the pony must be able to jump into a full gallop as soon as the starter's flag falls, and to stand without moving while the rider is performing a tricky manoeuvre.

A pony trained to respond to neck-reining can be guided and controlled with one hand while his rider is carrying items of equipment in the other.

Games training can take place almost anywhere – in a school, on a ride, with or without companions. General flatwork will improve suppleness, balance and

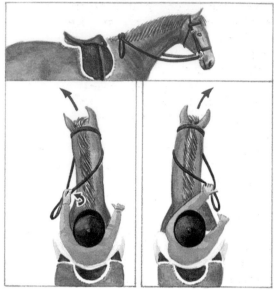

Neck-reining enables you to steer your pony with one hand. Knotting the reins *(top)* helps you to keep contact without any risk of trailing reins.

Many games call for you to **lead** your pony. If you try to drag him or look at him as you run, the pony becomes perverse, pulling back when you want him to keep up.

Instead, try to dismount before he stops so that he is still going forward and you can run alongside him, one hand on the rein to keep control.

obedience. Stopping, starting and neck-reining can be practised on a ride.

Never forget that the voice is an important aid. In gymkhanas, there are no rules against its use.

So teach your pony simple commands: *'Go!'* when you want him to move fast, using your heels and seat to urge him forwards; *'Stop!'*, reinforced by the aids to halt; *'Stand!'* when you want him to keep still. A clever pony soon gathers your meaning.

The pony must also be taught not to shy away from games equipment, especially flapping flags or sacks, brightly coloured cones and litter bins, waving wands and boxes or bottles that rattle. Here, the help of friends is very important. If you can get together for training, your ponies will soon cease to be amazed at anything you get up to!

Train your pony to get used to **flapping** items such as flags or sacks. A friend can help by providing the 'hazards'. Most ponies learn to take them in their stride.

Buckets and bins can be **noisy and alarming.** Never ride straight at an object: a pony's forward vision is limited and he will cope better if he can see it at an angle.

In team games, it is natural for a pony to duck away if another pony is approaching at speed. At the **handover** try to keep ponies a safe distance apart.

Training the rider

Many young riders who are lucky enough to acquire or inherit an experienced games pony complain that they cannot keep up with him!

Very often, the rider is just not fit, supple or co-ordinated enough to match the pony's ability.

Fitness is the first priority. Luckily, most enthusiastic riders are happier riding or caring for their ponies than lazing around, and are used to taking exercise.

There are various suppling exercises which can be practised anywhere, either on foot or mounted, and if carried out daily will help to tone up muscles.

With the feet apart, bend from the waist first to the right, then to the left, repeating the movements ten times. Keeping the legs straight, touch your toes half a dozen times. Then, standing on one leg, bring your knee up to touch your forehead and carry out the exercise three times on each leg.

When mounted, touch your right toe with your right hand, and do the same exercise on the left side. Stand in the stirrups, steadying yourself with one hand on the pommel of the saddle, and stretch your body upwards.

Practise dismounting whilst on the move, making certain that you land facing forwards and start running as soon as you touch the ground. Many games call for accuracy, so practise placing a tennis ball on a cone or a mug on a bending pole. And if you want really to speed up your performance, learn how to vault on and off your pony. The drawings on the right analyse the movements step by step. Vaulting on may be difficult at first as timing is very important, but keep trying and you will soon get the knack.

STAGES OF THE VAULT

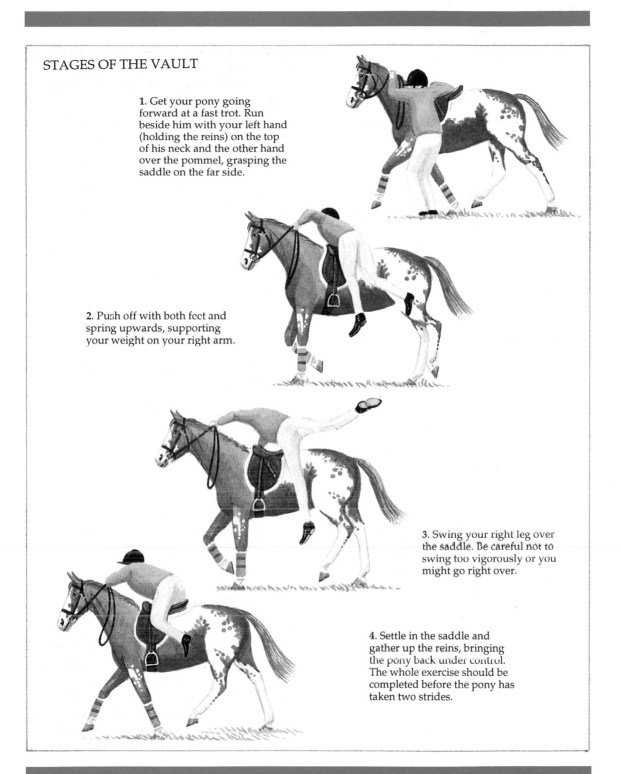

1. Get your pony going forward at a fast trot. Run beside him with your left hand (holding the reins) on the top of his neck and the other hand over the pommel, grasping the saddle on the far side.

2. Push off with both feet and spring upwards, supporting your weight on your right arm.

3. Swing your right leg over the saddle. Be careful not to swing too vigorously or you might go right over.

4. Settle in the saddle and gather up the reins, bringing the pony back under control. The whole exercise should be completed before the pony has taken two strides.

The show scene

Here a flag race is taking place in a wide, spacious arena. This type of setting is ideal and is often found at important Pony Club and county games competitions: it has a good, flat field, strong barriers and plenty going on. At many shows, however, the games arena is tucked away, sometimes in a space too small for it, and you and your pony have to learn to adapt to the conditions. If you are keen to be really good

at mounted games, take time to watch first-class games players, especially in team events, where the fluidity and skill of the riding make the games look deceptively easy. The best games riders, however, have reached such a standard by regular training and practice, and their skills could be within your reach. If possible, join the games squad of your local Pony Club branch.

Speed games

Most mounted games can be divided roughly into two categories – speed games, in which rider and pony must get from one end of the arena to the other and back again as quickly as possible; and precision games, where an item of equipment must be picked up, carried or balanced on another.

Big ponies will always have the edge on small ponies where speed is the main criterion, especially where the rider is not required to remount. But, if you drop or upset an item, you will have to get off to correct your mistake. With a big pony, getting on again can waste time, which is why it is so important to learn and perfect the vault.

On a small pony, an athletic rider can pick up fallen equipment without dismounting at all.

BENDING RACE

Bending is one of the fastest games. By taking a wide turn on the last pole, you narrow the angle of approach as you start the return journey (see diagram).

ROPE RACE

Rope race, a popular team game, requires two riders to negotiate the bending poles side by side. One rider peels off at the end while the other picks up another team-mate.

TYRE RACE

Another team game – the **tyre race.** The mounted rider must not release the other pony until his rider is through the tyre and safely in control of his mount.

14

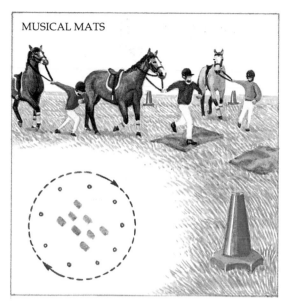

MUSICAL MATS

Musical mats is played like old-fashioned musical chairs. Riders dismount and lead their ponies to a mat when the music stops.

FLAG RACE

The **flag race** requires precision as well as speed. Hold the flag stick like a sword to place it in the cone. With practice, this manoeuvre can be carried out rapidly.

DRESSING-UP RACE

Dressing-up race, modern style. A versatile pony gets to the pile of clothes as quickly as possible, then waits patiently until the rider is ready to remount.

SACK RACE

The **sack race** calls for a swift approach to the sack and a rapid stop. A pony who leads well allows the rider to concentrate on keeping upright in the sack.

Precision games

The growing popularity of mounted games has made the organisers of gymkhanas ever more inventive.

All manner of everyday articles have found a new purpose – plastic bottles, tennis rackets, ice-cream cartons, old socks, even vacuum cleaner rings. One of the most versatile is the ubiquitous traffic cone, which can support a bending pole, balance a tennis ball or, in its cut-down version, carry several flags.

The importance of teaching your pony to neck-rein is emphasised in precision games where you usually have to carry a piece of equipment in one hand while guiding and controlling your pony with the other.

Practise at home, preferably with a friend, so that you can encourage each other. Learn to concentrate on the task involved so that you can keep mistakes to the minimum.

BALL AND CONE RACE

When placing a **ball** on a **cone**, approach the cone at an angle. Position the ball from directly above the cone, so that the pony's momentum does not dislodge the ball.

BALL AND BUCKET RACE

The closer you can get to the **bucket** the less chance there is of the **ball** bouncing out as you drop it in. Practise leaning down as far as you can before releasing the ball.

PYRAMID RACE

A tower of ice-cream cartons has to be built up in the **pyramid race**. This can be difficult to achieve unless your pony is under perfect control and his speed is checked.

LITTER RACE

This race involves picking up a piece of 'litter' on the end of a cane. Keep your hand low and use the pony's forward movement to bring the cane into the carrying position.

MUG RACE

Take care when placing a mug on a pole. It bounces off very easily. Because this race requires a number of tight turns, it is wise to fit studs to your pony's hind shoes.

EGG-AND-SPOON RACE

Few races need more concentration than the **egg-and-spoon**. An obedient pony who leads well is vital. Do not be tempted to 'secure' the egg with your thumb.

APPLE BOBBING

Anchor the apple on the bottom with your teeth. **Note:** Some organisers may provide wider buckets and will not allow you to remove your hat.

Making equipment

If you join a mounted games squad, you will be able to practise with other riders and use all the equipment that the trainer has gathered together. This is bound to be beneficial and will save some effort on your part, but making your own equipment for practising at home is not difficult.

Never throw anything away. The following items can all be used in mounted games: squash bottles, washing-up liquid containers, litter bins, old socks, tennis balls, broom handles, bamboo garden canes, paper and plastic sacks, fabric remnants. More elaborate equipment can be made from lengths of softwood, but here some skill in carpentry is required.

Some things will have to be bought. There is no substitute for traffic cones but these can be bought fairly cheaply from builders and road-mending suppliers.

Stuff the toe of an old sock with screwed-up newspaper. Roll up from the toe end and tuck in. A few stitches will help the 'ball' stand up to rough treatment.

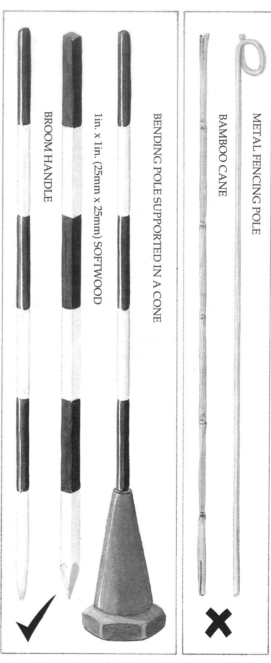

BROOM HANDLE

1in. x 1in. (25mm x 25mm) SOFTWOOD

BENDING POLE SUPPORTED IN A CONE

BAMBOO CANE

METAL FENCING POLE

Bending poles must be easily seen and tough. Broom handles and 4ft (120cm) lengths of softwood are excellent; bamboo canes and metal posts are dangerous.

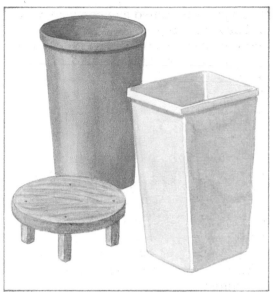

For a flag-holder, make a 'collar' from a strip of stiff paper 13ins (32cm) long (allowing 0.5in. (12mm) for the join), slip it over a cone and cut at the base of the collar.

Swing-top bins are useful accessories as they are the right height for use as tables. A table top can be made to fit inside the opening or the bin may be turned upside-down

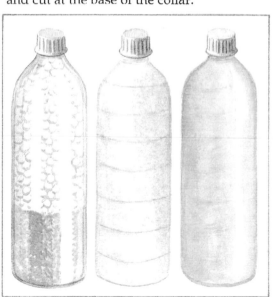

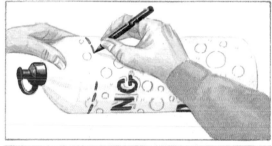

To give stability and substance to a plastic bottle, fill it one-third full of sand and top up with polystyrene beads. Cover with adhesive tape before painting.

'Litter' is made from 1-litre washing-up liquid bottles. The top of the bottle should be cut off just below the shoulder. Mark the line of the cut first.

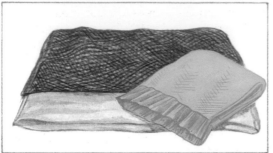

Sacks and bags have many uses. Hessian sacks are best for the sack race but are not easy to find. An old pillow-case is a handy bag where items have to be collected.

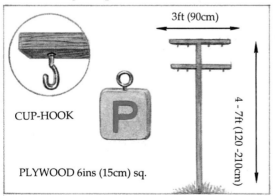

1.5-2ft (45-60cm) apart

Balloon-bursting is a popular Pony Club game. Balloon holders can be made by sewing clothes pegs 1.5-2ft (45-60cm) apart on a rectangular piece of hessian.

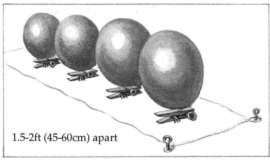

CUP-HOOK

P

3ft (90cm)

4 - 7ft (120 -210cm)

PLYWOOD 6ins (15cm) sq.

Some games call for a 'gallows' on which wooden letters or rings must be hung. Softwood and cup-hooks are used to make the gallows; plywood is best for letters.

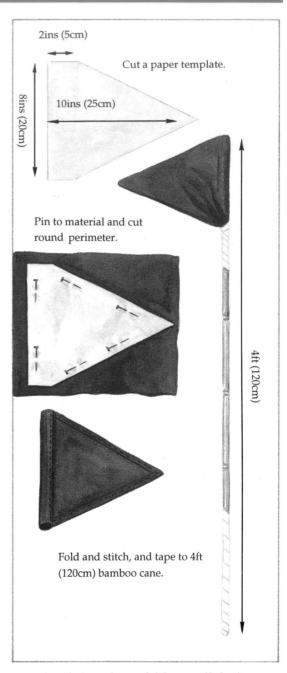

2ins (5cm)

Cut a paper template.

8ins (20cm)

10ins (25cm)

Pin to material and cut round perimeter.

4ft (120cm)

Fold and stitch, and tape to 4ft (120cm) bamboo cane.

Any brightly-coloured fabric will do for flags. The flags should be cut to shape as shown, hemmed and attached to 4ft (120cm) bamboo canes. Secure with insulating tape.

Games abroad

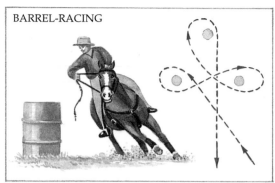

BARREL-RACING

In **barrel-racing**, the barrels are set out as shown. Riders race against the clock, coming in wide to the barrel and going away close, taking care not to rap the barrel.

POLE-BENDING — STAKE-RACING

For both **pole-bending** and **stake-racing**, straight runs to and from the last pole are involved. Stake-racing is usually a knock-out contest between two competitors.

In all countries where the European style of riding is practised, mounted games have become very popular, mainly due to the influence of the Pony Club, which organises international competitions.

In Western America, however, other types of games are held, mostly based on the special attributes of stock and trail horses. These include stamina, the ability to produce short bursts of speed, sudden stops and turns, and obedience to neck-reining.

The most famous of these games is barrel-racing in which riders compete against the clock. There are also variations of bending, known as pole-bending or, particularly in Australia, the stake race.

In some competitions, riders must obey the judge's commands, such as 'Back up!', 'Canter!' or 'Walk!'

Tent-pegging events, for adults and young riders, are held regularly in countries like Zimbabwe, Canada, South Africa and Australia.

TENT PEGGING

In **tent-pegging** contests, the peg is wooden and the 8-9ft (250-275cm) lance is made of aluminium with a razor-sharp point. The rider must spear the peg at a gallop, and let the lance follow through *(centre)* before bringing it back to the carry position *(right)*. Pace and style as well as capturing the peg all earn points.

Ready for competition

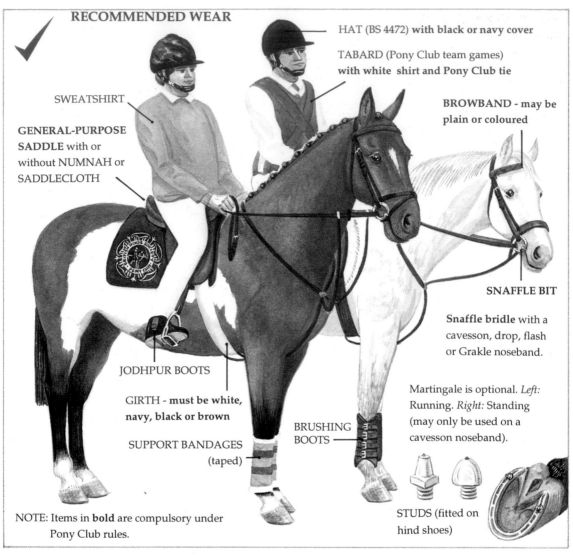

RECOMMENDED WEAR

HAT (BS 4472) **with black or navy cover**

TABARD (Pony Club team games) **with white shirt and Pony Club tie**

SWEATSHIRT

GENERAL-PURPOSE SADDLE with or without NUMNAH or SADDLECLOTH

BROWBAND - may be plain or coloured

SNAFFLE BIT

Snaffle bridle with a cavesson, drop, flash or Grakle noseband.

JODHPUR BOOTS

GIRTH - **must be white, navy, black or brown**

Martingale is optional. *Left:* Running. *Right:* Standing (may only be used on a cavesson noseband).

BRUSHING BOOTS

SUPPORT BANDAGES (taped)

STUDS (fitted on hind shoes)

NOTE: Items in **bold** are compulsory under Pony Club rules.

In Pony Club and county competitions, rules governing tack and dress are laid down, and riders can be prevented from taking part if the regulations are contravened.

Informal gymkhanas tend to be less strict, but it is always wise when entering a competition to check with the organisers beforehand.

These pages show the rights and wrongs of clothing and saddlery. In some cases, the rules are quite clear – you are **never** allowed to carry a whip or wear spurs in a gymkhana ring, you **must** wear a hat that conforms to British Standard 4472 and, in Pony Club competitions your pony **must** be ridden in a snaffle bridle.

Other 'wrongs' do not necessarily break any rules but if you commit them you would be putting yourself at a

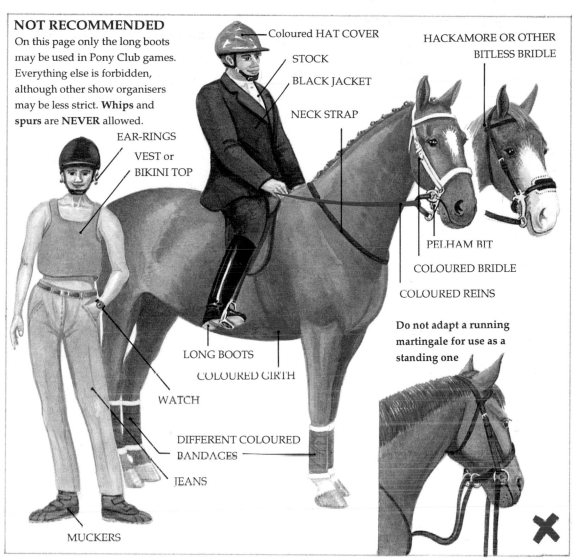

NOT RECOMMENDED

On this page only the long boots may be used in Pony Club games. Everything else is forbidden, although other show organisers may be less strict. **Whips** and **spurs** are **NEVER** allowed.

EAR-RINGS

VEST or BIKINI TOP

Coloured HAT COVER

STOCK

BLACK JACKET

NECK STRAP

HACKAMORE OR OTHER BITLESS BRIDLE

PELHAM BIT

COLOURED BRIDLE

COLOURED REINS

Do not adapt a running martingale for use as a standing one

LONG BOOTS

COLOURED GIRTH

WATCH

DIFFERENT COLOURED BANDAGES

JEANS

MUCKERS

disadvantage. Full length riding boots, for example, are not forbidden but you would find them very restricting. Most games enthusiasts wear jodhpur boots. Jackets, too, can be constricting; a tidy sweat shirt or jersey would be better.

Support bandages or brushing boots will protect your pony's legs and, if the ground is likely to be slippery, it is wise to fit studs in his hind shoes to help him

keep his footing.

Your pony should always be well turned out, but there is no need to plait. Some competitions are preceded by a tack inspection with rosettes awarded for turn-out. The judges are looking for clean saddles and bridles in good repair, so always check that the stitching is not coming undone, that buckles are sound and that leather is not cracked or split.

The day of the show

Getting your pony ready for a games event is just like preparing him for any other competition. He should be clean and tidy, and calm and confident – just like you.

Most games ponies, being of native stock, live out. If you can stable your pony the night before, so much the better, as he will get less dirty in a stable than in a muddy field. Wash the white areas if necessary, and groom him carefully.

On the evening before, gather together everything you will need for the show – it saves time in the morning.

At the end of the day, when both of you are tired – and, it is hoped, successful – the best thing you can do for a field-kept pony is to turn him out. A good roll is just the tonic he needs. Afterwards, he will look for a drink and then you can give him his supper.

If you wash your pony before the show, use a proprietary shampoo, rinse properly and dry carefully. Pay particular attention to the heels and do not let them get wet.

Even for a gymkhana, a pony needs a formidable amount of equipment. Carry everything except the haynet in the car and pack the car before loading the pony.

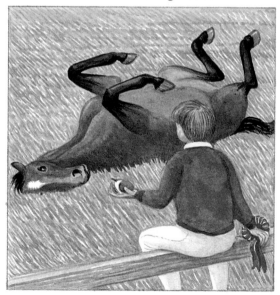

End of the day. Rolling is the way a pony unwinds and is usually the first thing he does when turned out into his field. Afterwards, he will settle to his supper.